BOAS, PYTHONS, AND ANACONDAS

BY: ERIC ETHAN

AN IMAGINATION LIBRARY SERIES

Gareth Stevens Publishing
MILWAUKEE

For a free color catalog describing Gareth Stevens' list of high-quality books, call 1-800-542-2595 (USA) or 1-800-461-9120 (Canada). Gareth Stevens' Fax: 1-414-225-0377.

Library of Congress Cataloging-in-Publication Data

Ethan, Eric.
    Boas, pythons, and anacondas / by Eric Ethan.
       p. cm. — (Fangs! an imagination library series)
    Includes index.
    Summary: Describes what these constrictors look like, what
they eat, where they can be found, how they defend themselves, the
dangers they present, and the outlook for their future.
    ISBN 0-8368-1427-4
    1. Boidae—Juvenile literature. [1. Boa constrictor.
2. Pythons. 3. Anaconda. 4. Snakes.] I. Title. II. Series:
Ethan, Eric. Fangs! an imagination library series.
QL666.063E84   1995
597.96—dc20   95-4734

Published in 1995 by:
Gareth Stevens Publishing
1555 N RiverCenter Drive, Suite 201
Milwaukee WI 53212 USA

Original Text: Eric Ethan
Series Design: Shari Tikus
Cover Design: Karen Knutson
Photo Credits: Pages 5, 13, and 17 © Joe McDonald; Pages 7, 9, 11 © James Carmichael; Page 15 © Stan Osolinski; Page 19 © Brian Kenney; Page 21 © Gail Shumway

Printed in the United States of America
    4 5 6 7 8 9 99

TABLE OF CONTENTS

What Are They? 4
What Do They Look Like? 6
Where Are They Found? 8
Senses and Hunting 10
What Do They Eat? 14
Self-Defense 16
Snake Attack 18
Unusual Facts 20
The Future 22
Glossary 23
Index and Places to
Write for More Information 24

WHAT ARE THEY?

Boas, pythons, and anacondas are all members of the *Boidae* (BOYday) family. They are the largest snakes in the world. None of them are poisonous. These snakes all kill by **constriction**. This means they coil around their prey and squeeze. These snakes are also called constrictors.

Snake experts believe these snakes first appeared when dinosaurs lived. *Boidae* snakes have two lungs. Modern snakes have only one lung.

Anacondas, like this one from South America, can be over 20 feet (6 meters) long.

WHAT DO THEY LOOK LIKE?

Constrictors have flat blocky heads shaped like a rectangle. They have thick necks and heavy bodies. Because they are not poisonous, none of these snakes have hollow fangs. But all of them have very sharp teeth they use to grip prey.

Their bodies are covered by flat, tough plates called scales. Constrictors must shed their skin to grow. First the old skin becomes dry and thin. Then a new skin forms and the snake crawls out of the old one.

Fully grown constrictors are very large. Boas, the smallest, reach 8-15 feet (2.5-4.5 meters). Pythons, the next largest, grow to 15-20 feet (4.5-6.0 meters). Anacondas are the biggest of all. An average size anaconda will weigh 250 pounds (112.5 kilos).

A red-tail boa from Peru showing a blocky head and thick body.

WHERE ARE THEY FOUND?

Boas live in the warm central parts of Africa and South America. Pythons are found mainly in Africa and Southeast Asia. The anaconda only lives in South America. All constrictors like water. Often they will lay in shallow water for hours. They can move much more quickly in water than on land.

Few people know that boa constrictors are native to North America. Both the rosy boa and rubber boa can be found in California and Arizona. Unlike most constrictors, these snakes live in dry areas.

Most constrictors do not make dens. Because they live where it is warm all year round they do not **hibernate**.

Garden tree boas like this one are found from Nicaragua to Peru.

SENSES AND HUNTING

Constrictors are **predators**. This means they must eat other animals to stay alive. Most snakes try to feed once a week. Constrictors feed only once every three weeks.

Constrictors cannot hear well or see very far. Their tongue helps them find prey. Each time it flicks out of the snake's mouth, it takes a sample of the air and ground around it. In the constrictor's mouth the **Jacobson's organ analyzes** what the tongue picks up. This tells the snake what is nearby.

This albino Burmese python is using its tongue to find prey.

Boas and pythons have several pits near their nose. These are called **labial pits**. These allow the snakes to find warm prey even at night.

Constrictors hunt on land mostly at night. It helps them hide their large size. In water they also hunt during the day.

Because they are so large and slow moving, constrictors ambush their prey. This means they wait in one place for a long time until an animal comes close enough to strike. In water these snakes can move much faster and will go after prey.

Can you see the labial pits on this green tree python?

WHAT DO THEY EAT?

Fully grown pythons and anacondas are very big and only eat once every three weeks. They hunt larger animals like goats, deer, and wild pigs. Young constrictors and tree boas eat birds and smaller animals like rats and mice. Anacondas will catch fish and small alligators.

Constrictors often kill animals bigger than they are. To swallow them, constrictors can stretch their mouths very wide. They also swallow prey head first to make it easier. A constrictor breathes through a tube that goes all the way to the tip of its mouth. This keeps it from choking when swallowing large animals.

This rock python of central Africa is eating an impala.

SELF-DEFENSE

Even though constrictors can be very large, they still use **camouflage** to hide from danger. In the rain forests and dense jungle where most of these snakes live, it can be hard to see them. Anacondas and pythons spend a lot of time in shallow water. They hide their bodies below the surface and leave just their heads sticking out.

Wild pigs and alligators will kill young constrictors, but fully grown constrictors have no enemies but humans. Their large size and great strength protect them from all other animals.

The blood python of Indonesia is well camouflaged.

SNAKE ATTACK

Even though they are very large and slow moving, constrictors can strike at prey very quickly. Constrictors try to grab animals by the head. They wrap their coils around them and squeeze.

Constrictors are not poisonous. They do not have fangs but they do have very sharp teeth. When they hunt they bite and hold on. Sometimes constrictors are bitten and badly hurt by animals they are hunting.

There are no definite cases where a constrictor has killed a human being. Anacondas and pythons over 15 feet (4.5 meters) are still very dangerous. They have large, sharp teeth and bite very hard. But most people can avoid a constrictor's coils.

A large reticulated python from Indonesia striking.

UNUSUAL FACTS

Pythons are sacred in parts of central Africa. Very old temples with snakes carved into the walls have been found there.

Boa constrictors are believed to be the longest lived snakes. Boas have lived over forty years in zoos.

The rosy boa, found in California and Arizona, rolls into a tight ball if danger is near. It pokes out its tail to confuse its enemies. The rosy boa and rubber boa are the only constrictors found in North America. They are so rare few people have ever seen one.

The biggest anaconda on record was almost 28 feet (8.5 meters) long. People in South America say that anacondas over 35 feet (11 meters) long live in the jungle.

This red-tail boa from Peru is constricting a mouse.

THE FUTURE

Loss of **habitat** is the biggest threat to constrictors. Rain forests in South America and jungles in Africa are being cleared for lumber or to create new areas for farming. Wet areas are sometimes drained for farming, too. This also reduces the number of animals the snakes feed on.

Pythons and anacondas are large enough that their skins are used by people. Shoes, belts, and other kinds of clothing are made from snake skins. It is not legal to bring some of these things into some countries. But that has not stopped the trade world wide.

GLOSSARY

analyze (AN a lize) - To separate something into its parts to study them.

camouflage (KAM 0 flazh) - Colors or patterns that help an animal look like the ground around it.

constriction (KON stric shun) - The squeezing of a snake's body when it kills prey.

habitat (HAB i tat) - The place where an animal is normally found.

hibernate (HI ber nate) - To spend the winter in a deep sleep.

labial pit (LAY be all) - Small holes above a snake's lip that can see infrared light.

Jacobson's organ (JAY kob sons OR gan) - A special pouch in a snake's mouth that analyzes what the tongue picks up.

predator (PRED a tor) - An animal that lives by killing and eating other animals.

INDEX

Africa 8, 20, 22
ambush 12
constrictors 4, 6, 8, 10, 12, 14, 16, 18, 20, 22
defense 16
fangs 6, 18
hunt 12, 14, 18
hearing 10
Jacobson's organ 10
Labial pit 12
lung 4

North America 20, 22
predator 10
prey 4, 6, 10, 12, 14, 18
rain forest 16, 22
scales 6
South America 8, 20, 22
Southeast Asia 8
strike 12, 18
tongue 10
water 8, 12, 16

PLACES TO WRITE FOR MORE INFORMATION

American Society of Ichthyologists and Herpetologists
US National Museum
Washington, DC 20560

Copeia
American Society of Herpetologists
34th Street and Girard Avenue
Philadelphia, PA 19104

Herpetologist's League
1041 New Hampshire Street
Lawrence, KS 66044

Herpetological
1041 New Hampshire Street
Lawrence, KS 66044